D0503846

THE
LITTLE BOOK OF
SELF-CARE
— FOR —
ARIES

Simple Ways to Refresh and
Restore—According
to the Stars

CONSTANCE STELLAS

ADAMS MEDIA

NEW YORK LONDON TORONTO SYDNEY NEW DELHI

Adams Media
An Imprint of Simon & Schuster, Inc.
100 Technology Center Drive
Stoughton, MA 02072

Copyright © 2019 by Simon & Schuster, Inc.

All rights reserved, including the right to reproduce this book or portions
thereof in any form whatsoever. For information address Adams Media
Subsidiary Rights Department, 1230 Avenue of the Americas, New York,
NY 10020.

First Adams Media hardcover edition January 2019

ADAMS MEDIA and colophon are trademarks of Simon & Schuster.

For information about special discounts for bulk purchases, please
contact Simon & Schuster Special Sales at 1-866-506-1949 or
business@simonandschuster.com.

The Simon & Schuster Speakers Bureau can bring authors to your live event. For more information or to book an event contact the Simon & Schuster Speakers
Bureau at 1-866-248-3049 or visit our website at www.simonspeakers.com.

Interior design by Sylvia McArdle
Interior images © Getty Images; Clipart.com

Manufactured in the United States of America

6 2022

Library of Congress Cataloging-in-Publication Data
Names: Stellas, Constance, author.
Title: The little book of self-care for Aries / Constance Stellas.
Description: Avon, Massachusetts: Adams Media, 2019.
Series: Astrology self-care.
Identifiers: LCCN 2018038278 | ISBN 9781507209646 (hc) | ISBN 9781507209653 (ebook)
Subjects: LCSH: Aries (Astrology) | Self-care, Health--Miscellanea.
Classification: LCC BF1727 .S74 2019 | DDC 133.3/22--dc23
LC record available at https://urldefense.proofpoint.com/v2/url?u=https-3A_lccn.loc.gov
_2018038278&d=DwIFAg&c=jGUuvAdBXp_VqQ6toyah2g&r=eLFfdQgpHVWoiSAzG8F-WtS-
jrFvCD9jGMJBHtzyExXhmHvwB7sjMCnFuKz95Uyqa&m=d8ZpCPiE6ogChQ9yrWyRZidjNRY-
DdBr7svcu19nRAYA&s=vpTIVRYKIOyCH3mCfrSE3_zSKz1ZpufCzcYJ7e2UPus&e=

ISBN 978-1-5072-0964-6
ISBN 978-1-5072-0965-3 (ebook)

Many of the designations used by manufacturers and sellers to distinguish their products are
claimed as trademarks. Where those designations appear in this book and Simon & Schuster,
Inc., was aware of a trademark claim, the designations have been printed with initial capital
letters.

This book is intended as general information only, and should not be used to diagnose or treat
any health condition. In light of the complex, individual, and specific nature of health problems, this book is not intended to replace professional medical advice. The ideas, procedures,
and suggestions in this book are intended to supplement, not replace, the advice of a trained
medical professional. Consult your physician before adopting any of the suggestions in this
book, as well as about any condition that may require diagnosis or medical attention. The author and publisher disclaim any liability arising directly or indirectly from the use of this book.

Dedication

To my impetuous Aries friends,
who get things going.

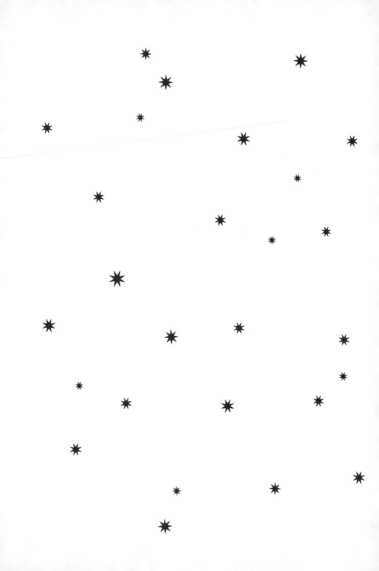

CONTENTS

Acknowledgments

I would like to thank Karen Cooper and everyone at Adams Media who helped with this book. To Brendan O'Neill, Katie Corcoran Lytle, Laura Daly, Julia Jacques, Eileen Mullan, Sarah Doughty, Meredith O'Hayre, Casey Ebert, Sylvia Davis, and everyone else who worked on the manuscripts. To Frank Rivera, Colleen Cunningham, and Katrina Machado for their work on the book's cover and interior design. I appreciated your team spirit and eagerness to dive into the riches of astrology.

Introduction

It's time for you to have a little *"me" time*—powered by the zodiac. By tapping into your Sun sign's astrological and elemental energies, *The Little Book of Self-Care for Aries* brings star-powered strength and cosmic relief to your life with self-care guidance tailored specifically for you.

You are blessed with passionate determination, Aries, and this book focuses on your true self. This book provides information on how to incorporate self-care into your life while teaching you just how important astrology is to your overall self-care routine. You'll learn more about yourself as you learn about your sign and its governing element, fire. Then you can relax, rejuvenate, and stay balanced with more than one hundred self-care ideas and activities perfect for your Aries personality.

From a refreshing run to a calming foot massage, you will find plenty of ways to heal your mind, body, and active spirit. Now, let the stars be your self-care guide!

♈

PART 1

SIGNS,
ELEMENTS,
— AND —
SELF-CARE

CHAPTER 1

WHAT IS SELF-CARE?

✳

Astrology gives insights into whom to love, when to charge forward into new beginnings, and how to succeed in whatever you put your mind to. When paired with self-care, astrology can also help you relax and reclaim that part of yourself that tends to get lost in the bustle of the day. In this chapter you'll learn what self-care is—for you. (No matter your sign, self-care is more than just lit candles and quiet reflection, though these activities may certainly help you find the renewal that you seek.) You'll also learn how making a priority of personalized self-care activities can benefit you in ways you may not even have thought of. Whether you're a Leo, a Pisces, or a Taurus, you deserve rejuvenation and renewal that's customized to your sign—this chapter reveals where to begin.

What Self-Care Is

Self-care is any activity that you do to take care of yourself. It rejuvenates your body, refreshes your mind, or realigns your spirit. It relaxes and refuels you. It gets you ready for a new day or a fresh start. It's the practices, rituals, and meaningful activities that you do, just for you, that help you feel safe, grounded, happy, and fulfilled.

The activities that qualify as self-care are amazingly unique and personalized to who you are, what you like, and, in large part, what your astrological sign is. If you're asking questions about what self-care practices are best for those ruled by fire and born under the energetic eye of Aries, you'll find answers—and restoration—in Part 2. But, no matter which of those self-care activities speak to you and your unique place in the universe on any given day, it will fall into one of the following self-care categories—each of which pertains to a different aspect of your life:

* Physical self-care
* Emotional self-care
* Social self-care
* Mental self-care
* Spiritual self-care
* Practical self-care

When you practice all of these unique types of self-care—and prioritize your practice to ensure you are choosing the best options for your unique sign and governing element—know that you are actively working to create the version of yourself that the universe intends you to be.

Physical Self-Care

When you practice physical self-care, you make the decision to look after and restore the one physical body that has been bestowed upon you. Care for it. Use it in the best way you can imagine, for that is what the universe wishes you to do. You can't light the world on fire or move mountains if you're not doing everything you can to take care of your physical health.

Emotional Self-Care

Emotional self-care is when you take the time to acknowledge and care for your inner self, your emotional well-being. Whether you're angry or frustrated, happy or joyful, or somewhere in between, emotional self-care happens when you choose to sit with your emotions: when you step away from the noise of daily life that often drowns out or tamps down your authentic self. Emotional self-care lets you see your inner you as the cosmos intend. Once you identify your true emotions, you can either accept them and continue to move forward on your journey or you can try to change any negative emotions for the better. The more you acknowledge your feelings and practice emotional self-care, the more you'll feel the positivity that the universe and your life holds for you.

Social Self-Care

You practice social self-care when you nurture your relationships with others, be they friends, coworkers, or family members. In today's hectic world it's easy to let relationships fall to the wayside, but it's so important to share your life with others—and let others share their lives with you. Social self-care is reciprocal and often karmic. The support and love that you put out into the universe through social self-care is given back to you by those you socialize with—often tenfold.

Mental Self-Care

Mental self-care is anything that keeps your mind working quickly and critically. It helps you cut through the fog of the day, week, or year and ensures that your quick wit and sharp mind are intact and working the way the cosmos intended. Making sure your mind is fit helps you problem-solve, decreases stress since you're not feeling overwhelmed, and keeps you feeling on top of your mental game—no matter your sign or your situation.

Spiritual Self-Care

Spiritual self-care is self-care that allows you to tap into your soul and the soul of the universe and uncover its secrets. Rather than focusing on a particular religion or set of religious beliefs, these types of self-care activities reconnect you with a higher power: the sense that something out there is bigger than you. When you meditate, you connect. When you pray, you connect. Whenever you do something that allows you to experience and marry yourself to the vastness that is the cosmos, you practice spiritual self-care.

Practical Self-Care

Self-care is what you do to take care of yourself, and practical self-care, while not as expansive as the other types, is made up of the seemingly small day-to-day tasks that bring you peace and accomplishment. These practical self-care rituals are important, but are often overlooked. Scheduling a doctor's appointment that you've been putting off is practical self-care. Getting your hair cut is practical self-care. Anything you can check off your list of things to be accomplished gives you a sacred space to breathe and allows the universe more room to bring a beautiful sense of cosmic fulfillment your way.

What Self-Care Isn't

Self-care is restorative. Self-care is clarifying. Self-care is whatever you need to do to make yourself feel secure in the universe.

Now that you know what self-care is, it's also important that you're able to see what self-care isn't. Self-care is not something that you force yourself to do because you think it will be good for you. Some signs are energy in motion and sitting still goes against their place in the universe. Those signs won't feel refreshed by lying in a hammock or sitting down to meditate. Other signs aren't able to ground themselves unless they've found a self-care practice that protects their cosmic need for peace and quiet. Those signs won't find parties, concerts, and loud venues soothing or satisfying. If a certain ritual doesn't bring you peace, clarity, or satisfaction, then it's not right for your sign and you should find something that speaks to you more clearly.

There's a difference though between not finding satisfaction in a ritual that you've tried and not wanting to try a self-care activity because you're tired or stuck in a comfort zone. Sometimes going to the gym or meeting up with friends is the self-care practice that you need to experience—whether engaging in it feels like a downer or not. So consider how you feel when you're actually doing the activity. If it feels invigorating to get on the treadmill or you feel delight when you actually catch up with your friend, the ritual is doing what it should be doing and clearing space for you—among other benefits...

The Benefits of Self-Care

The benefits of self-care are boundless and there's none that's superior to helping you put rituals in place to feel more at home in your body, in your spirit, and in your unique home in the cosmos. There are, however, other benefits to engaging in the practice of self-care that you should know.

Rejuvenates Your Immune System

No matter which rituals are designated for you by the stars, your sign, and its governing element, self-care helps both your body and mind rest, relax, and recuperate. The practice of self-care activates the parasympathetic nervous system (often called the rest and digest system), which slows your heart rate, calms the body, and overall helps your body relax and release tension. This act of decompression gives your body the space it needs to build up and strengthen your immune system, which protects you from illness.

Helps You Reconnect—with Yourself

When you practice the ritual of self-care—especially when you customize this practice based on your personal sign and governing element—you learn what you like to do and what you need to do to replenish yourself. Knowing yourself better, and allowing yourself the time and space that you need to focus on your personal needs and desires, gives you the gifts of self-confidence and self-knowledge. Setting time aside to focus on your needs also helps you put busy, must-do things aside, which gives you time to reconnect with yourself and who you are deep inside.

Increases Compassion

Perhaps one of the most important benefits of creating a self-care ritual is that, by focusing on yourself, you become more compassionate to others as well. When you truly take the time to care for yourself and make yourself and your importance in the universe a priority in your own life, you're then able to care for others and see their needs and desires in a new way. You can't pour from an empty dipper, and self-care allows you the space and clarity to do what you can to send compassion out into the world.

Starting a Self-Care Routine

Self-care should be treated as a ritual in your life, something you make the time to pause for, no matter what. You are important. You deserve rejuvenation and a sense of relaxation. You need to open your soul to the gifts that the universe is giving you, and self-care provides you with a way to ensure you're ready to receive those gifts. To begin a self-care routine, start by making yourself the priority. Do the customized rituals in Part 2 with intention, knowing the universe has already given them to you, by virtue of your sign and your governing element.

Now that you understand the role that self-care will hold in your life, let's take a closer look at the connection between self-care and astrology.

CHAPTER 2

SELF-CARE AND ASTROLOGY

Astrology is the study of the connection between the objects in the heavens (the planets, the stars) and what happens here on earth. Just as the movements of the planets and other heavenly bodies influence the ebb and flow of the tides, so do they influence you—your body, your mind, your spirit. This relationship is ever present and is never more important—or personal—than when viewed through the lens of self-care.

In this chapter you'll learn how the locations of these celestial bodies at the time of your birth affect you and define the self-care activities that will speak directly to you as an Aries, a Leo, a Capricorn, or any of the other zodiac signs. You'll see how the zodiac influences every part of your being and why ignoring its lessons can leave you feeling frustrated and unfulfilled. You'll also realize that, when you perform the rituals of self-care based on your sign, the wisdom of the cosmos will lead you down a path of fulfillment and restoration—to the return of who *you* really are, deep inside.

Zodiac Polarities

In astrology, all signs are mirrored by other signs that are on the opposite side of the zodiac. This polarity ensures that the zodiac is balanced and continues to flow with an unbreakable, even stream of energy. There are two different polarities in the zodiac and each is called by a number of different names:

* Yang/masculine/positive polarity
* Yin/feminine/negative polarity

Each polar opposite embodies a number of opposing traits, qualities, and attributes that will influence which self-care practices will work for or against your sign and your own personal sense of cosmic balance.

Yang

Whether male or female, those who fall under yang, or masculine, signs are extroverted and radiate their energy outward. They are spontaneous, active, bold, and fearless. They move forward in life with the desire to enjoy everything the world has to offer to them, and they work hard to transfer their inspiration and positivity to others so that those individuals may experience the same gifts that the universe offers them.

All signs governed by the fire and air elements are yang and hold the potential for these dominant qualities. We will refer to them with masculine pronouns. These signs are:

* Aries
* Leo
* Sagittarius

* Gemini
* Libra
* Aquarius

There are people who hold yang energy who are introverted and retiring. However, by practicing self-care that is customized for your sign and understanding the potential ways to use your energy, you can find a way—perhaps one that's unique to you—to claim your native buoyancy and dominance and engage with the path that the universe opens for you.

Yin

Whether male or female, those who fall under yin, or feminine, signs are introverted and radiate inwardly. They draw people and experiences to them rather than seeking people and experiences in an extroverted way. They move forward in life with an energy that is reflective, receptive, and focused on communication and achieving shared goals. All signs governed by the earth and water elements are yin and hold the potential for these reflective qualities. We will refer to them with feminine pronouns. These signs are:

* Taurus
* Virgo
* Capricorn

* Cancer
* Scorpio
* Pisces

As there are people with yang energy who are introverted and retiring, there are also people with yin energy who are outgoing and extroverted. And by practicing self-care rituals that speak to your particular sign, energy, and governing body, you will reveal your true self and the balance of energy will be maintained.

Governing Elements

Each astrological sign has a governing element that defines their energy orientation and influences both the way the sign moves through the universe and relates to self-care. The elements are fire, earth, air, and water. All the signs in each element share certain characteristics, along with having their own sign-specific qualities:

* **Fire:** Fire signs are adventurous, bold, and energetic. They enjoy the heat and warm environments and look to the sun and fire as a means to recharge their depleted batteries. They're competitive, outgoing, and passionate. The fire signs are Aries, Leo, and Sagittarius.
* **Earth:** Earth signs all share a common love and tendency toward a practical, material, sensual, and economic orientation. The earth signs are Taurus, Virgo, and Capricorn.
* **Air:** Air is the most ephemeral element and those born under this element are thinkers, innovators, and communicators. The air signs are Gemini, Libra, and Aquarius.
* **Water:** Water signs are instinctual, compassionate, sensitive, and emotional. The water signs are Cancer, Scorpio, and Pisces.

Chapter 3 teaches you all about the ways your specific governing element influences and drives your connection to your cosmically harmonious self-care rituals, but it's important that you realize how important these elemental traits are to your self-care practice and to the activities that will help restore and reveal your true self.

Sign Qualities

Each of the astrological elements governs three signs. Each of these three signs is also given its own quality or mode, which corresponds to a different part of each season: the beginning, the middle, or the end.

* **Cardinal signs:** The cardinal signs initiate and lead in each season. Like something that is just starting out, they are actionable, enterprising, and assertive, and are born leaders. The cardinal signs are Aries, Cancer, Libra, and Capricorn.
* **Fixed signs:** The fixed signs come into play when the season is well established. They are definite, consistent, reliable, motivated by principles, and powerfully stubborn. The fixed signs are Taurus, Leo, Scorpio, and Aquarius.
* **Mutable signs:** The mutable signs come to the forefront when the seasons are changing. They are part of one season, but also part of the next. They are adaptable, versatile, and flexible. The mutable signs are Gemini, Virgo, Sagittarius, and Pisces.

Each of these qualities tells you a lot about yourself and who you are. They also give you invaluable information about the types of self-care rituals that your sign will find the most intuitive and helpful.

Ruling Planets

In addition to qualities and elements, each specific sign is ruled by a particular planet that lends its personality to those born under that sign. Again, these sign-specific traits give you valuable insight into the personality of the signs and the self-care rituals that may best rejuvenate them. The signs that correspond to each planet—and the ways that those planetary influences determine your self-care options—are as follows:

* **Aries:** Ruled by Mars, Aries is passionate, energetic, and determined.
* **Taurus:** Ruled by Venus, Taurus is sensual, romantic, and fertile.
* **Gemini:** Ruled by Mercury, Gemini is intellectual, changeable, and talkative.
* **Cancer:** Ruled by the Moon, Cancer is nostalgic, emotional, and home loving.
* **Leo:** Ruled by the Sun, Leo is fiery, dramatic, and confident.
* **Virgo:** Ruled by Mercury, Virgo is intellectual, analytical, and responsive.
* **Libra:** Ruled by Venus, Libra is beautiful, romantic, and graceful.
* **Scorpio:** Ruled by Mars and Pluto, Scorpio is intense, powerful, and magnetic.
* **Sagittarius:** Ruled by Jupiter, Sagittarius is optimistic, boundless, and larger than life.
* **Capricorn:** Ruled by Saturn, Capricorn is wise, patient, and disciplined.

* **Aquarius:** Ruled by Uranus, Aquarius is independent, unique, and eccentric.
* **Pisces:** Ruled by Neptune and Jupiter, Pisces is dreamy, sympathetic, and idealistic.

A Word on Sun Signs

When someone is a Leo, Aries, Sagittarius, or any of the other zodiac signs, it means that the sun was positioned in this constellation in the heavens when they were born. Your Sun sign is a dominant factor in defining your personality, your best self-care practices, and your soul nature. Every person also has the position of the Moon, Mercury, Venus, Mars, Jupiter, Saturn, Uranus, Neptune, and Pluto. These planets can be in any of the elements: fire signs, earth signs, air signs, or water signs. If you have your entire chart calculated by an astrologer or on an Internet site, you can see the whole picture and learn about all your elements. Someone born under Leo with many signs in another element will not be as concentrated in the fire element as someone with five or six planets in Leo. Someone born in Pisces with many signs in another element will not be as concentrated in the water element as someone with five or six planets in Pisces. And so on. Astrology is a complex system and has many shades of meaning. For our purposes looking at the self-care practices designated by your Sun sign, or what most people consider their sign, will give you the information you need to move forward and find fulfillment and restoration.

CHAPTER 3

ESSENTIAL ELEMENTS: FIRE

✳

F ire gives us heat, warmth, and light. And those who have fire as their governing element—like you, Aries, as well as Leo and Sagittarius—all have a special energy signature and connection with fire that guides all aspects of their lives. Fire signs are drawn to the flames in all its varied forms and environments whether this gift comes from the sun, an outdoor campfire, or a cozy fireplace fire, and their approach to self-care reflects their relationship with this fiery element. Let's take a look at the mythological importance of the sun, as well as the basic characteristics of the three fire signs, and what they all have in common when it comes to self-care.

The Mythology of Fire

In astrology, fire is considered the first element of creation. Perhaps it was primitive man's way of understanding the big bang, or maybe fire just made a clear-cut difference between living in the wild and gathering together in human communities. In Greek mythology the immortal Prometheus angered the gods by stealing fire for the mortals he had such affection for down on earth. As punishment he was chained to a rock and Zeus sent an eagle to eat his liver. Magically, this liver regenerated every day and the eagle kept devouring it. Prometheus was later released from this curse, but the gift of fire that he gave to mankind was not completely free of conflict.

Fire was—and remains—an essential part of civilized life, but it also gives humans the ability to forge weapons of war. Fire warms a home, cooks a meal, and restores and enlivens the spirit, but too much fire can destroy. All fire signs feel this duality between the creative and destructive force of their fire power energy, and this duality drives their likes and dislikes, personality traits, and approaches to self-care.

The Element of Fire

The fire signs are known as the inspirational signs because their enthusiasm and buoyant personalities help them to cheer themselves and others on to great success. They also represent the spiritual side of human nature and their sense of intuition is strong; fire signs often have hunches about themselves and others, and if they follow these hunches, they typically achieve whatever they set out to do. For example, Aries inspires the spark that pioneers a project or endeavor. Leo is a leader who inspires his circle of friends, family, or colleagues to keep their eyes on the goal at hand, even when things get tough. And Sagittarius is an idealist and searches (and helps others search) for truth.

Astrological Symbols

The astrological symbols (also called the zodiacal symbols) of the fire signs also give you hints as to how the fire signs move through the world. All of the fire signs are represented by animals of power and determination, which ties right back to their shared fiery element:

* Aries is the Ram
* Leo is the Lion
* Sagittarius is the Centaur (half horse/half man)

Each fire sign's personality and subsequent approaches to self-care connect to the qualities of these representative animals. For example, the Ram is determined and confident. The Lion is king of the jungle and boldly defends his turf. And the Centaur, also called the Archer, shoots his arrows of truth and moves powerfully against any attempts to rein him in.

Signs and Seasonal Modes

Each of the elements in astrology has a sign that corresponds to a different part of each season.

* **Cardinal:** Aries, as the first fire sign, is the harbinger of spring, and the spring equinox begins the astrological year. Aries is called a cardinal fire sign because it leads the season.

* **Fixed:** Leo, the second fire sign, occurs in midsummer when summer is well established. Leo is a fixed fire sign. The fixed signs are definite, motivated by principles, and powerfully stubborn.
* **Mutable:** Sagittarius is the sign that brings us from one season to the next. Sagittarius moves us from autumn to winter. These signs are called mutable. In terms of character the mutable signs are changeable and flexible.

If you know your element and whether you are a cardinal, fixed, or mutable sign, you know a lot about yourself. This is invaluable for self-care and is reflected in the customized fire sign self-care rituals found in Part 2.

Fire Signs and Self-Care

Self-care is incredibly important for fire signs. But learning how to set aside time for self-care takes discipline because fire doesn't want to stop. Fire elements have a wonderful spark that lights up their minds, bodies, and spirits, but, as with fire, those born under this element frequently burn out. When this happens, making frequent pit stops to refuel, rest, and engage in self-care activities that are personalized for their element—like the ones found in Part 2—are what fire signs require to be stoked back to life.

Fire signs need to keep in mind that their self-care activities should be fun and varied; they don't want to get bored doing the same thing over and over again when there are so many different self-care options to try! The fire element crackles with enthusiasm and good spirits, and the more activity, socializing, and fun they can have, the better they like it and the easier it is for people born under this element to get fired up. Fire signs will easily follow any practice or activity that enhances playfulness. Variety in exercise, diet, décor, fashion, friendship, vacations, and socializing gives all fire elements the motivation to enjoy life, and without a good time life is a misery for these bold personalities.

The best way to approach self-care for fire signs is to make it a game. The fire signs have willpower to follow through on a plan if they decide something is worthwhile and they can enjoy it. The rules of the "game" don't matter as much as the sense of achieving a good score, beating the competition, or enjoying the process. For example, if a fire sign decides to do 10,000 steps in a day and finds at 5 p.m. that he is 1,000 steps short, his motivation to reach his goal would help him find a fun way to complete the program. Perhaps he will decide to march to music, skip, or hop his way to 10,000. A fire sign will get what he needs in two different ways through this type of self-care: he both wins the game and has fun doing it!

Maintaining that flame and steady inspiration is the goal of any self-care program. Play the game of taking care of your body, mind, and spirit, and not only will you benefit from your efforts, but you will also inspire others to follow you.

So now that you know what fire signs need to practice self-care, let's look at each of the fiery characteristics of Aries and how he can maintain his flame.

CHAPTER 4

SELF-CARE FOR ARIES

Dates: March 21–April 19
Element: Fire
Polarity: Yang
Quality: Cardinal
Symbol: Ram
Ruler: Mars

Not only is your sign, Aries, the first fire sign, it is also the first sign of the zodiac. The astrological calendar begins with the vernal equinox (usually about March 21), and all of the astrological signs are calculated from this date, which is called the Aries Ingress. The vernal equinox also marks the beginning of the renewal holidays of Easter and Passover, which is interesting when you consider that the image of the Ram or Paschal Lamb figures strongly in both the Jewish and Christian traditions. The Ram, with his beautiful curled horns, is also Aries's symbol. The ram was also identified with the Egyptian god Ammon, and in Greek mythology Phrixus sacrificed the Golden Fleece, the fleece of a winged gold ram, to Zeus. As a reward for this sacrifice, Zeus placed the ram in the heavens as the constellation Aries.

In Greek mythology the god of war was Ares, and he was known for his hot temper, aggressive fighting, and skills in weaponry. In Roman mythology his name was Mars. Although he had a quieter and more complex reputation than Ares, he was still ruled by the red planet.

Like all fire signs Aries is an extrovert and delights in expressing his power. Each of the four cardinal signs of the zodiac that begin the seasons are very active, but Aries leads the group in terms of the sheer amount of energy he has available. However, Aries's energy is not concentrated, nor can it be easily tamed. He tends to begin many projects but complete few. As soon as his enthusiasm wanes, he is on to another idea or quest. The challenge for this sign in life and in terms of self-care is containing and channeling his fiery gift.

As the first sign Aries is just beginning to develop his personality and soul qualities. This childlike enthusiasm that Aries has is the source of his energy. He is boundlessly interested in seeing what he can do in the world and thrives on variety and activity. He delights in expressing himself. Aries is self-centered in a charming but sometimes abrasive way. These are not negative soul qualities, just Aries's energy playing with the fire of creation. For others who are not filled with this spirit, Aries can be very irritating. He is impatient and quick to anger, and has no qualms in walking out of a room when bored or disenchanted with something. Aries in the main cannot be directed.

An Aries can become a timid sheep, but the spark of an idea or project that really interests him is enough to fan the flames and get him back to his fire power. A subdued Aries needs to be encouraged. He is trying to balance his native energy with an imposed idea of what would be nice or good. This problem can be especially pronounced with a female Aries, as she feels the yang fire but might be reluctant to express it for fear of not being perceived as feminine. This dichotomy was more pronounced in other generations, but the split can still exist today. Fortunately, there are now many ways that the Aries girl or woman can assertively express herself.

Self-Care and Aries

Aries rarely thinks about taking care of himself until something sidelines him. Perhaps it is an injury or illness, as Aries can be accident prone. When and if such a bump occurs, the best way for Aries to get back on track is an appeal to his sense of competition and physical fitness. Aries needs a healthy body that can respond to his energy demands—and he needs it right away. Aries usually heals very quickly because he is so impatient. He is also inspired by the spiritual gains of a healthy mind, body, and spirit. His intuition works much better when he is healthy.

The best way to approach self-care for Aries is to make the program quick. Using apps to monitor exercise, calories, and any other measurement of health is a good way to get Aries keen on taking care of himself. If Aries decides to go on a diet, his first step is to find a program with food that tastes flavorful. Tabasco sauce, garlic powder, and horseradish are Aries ruled and can keep his taste buds engaged while he sheds pounds.

Aries Rules the Head

Each zodiac sign rules a part of the body. Aries rules the head, skull, face, and sinus passages, which relates to his head-strong nature. It is especially important for Aries to protect this vulnerable area of the body. However, it may take a few near collisions or accidents to convince Aries that headgear is important. He prefers to be free and only experience will encourage him to pursue safety first.

Aries can suffer from headaches, which are usually a sign that he is damming up his vital energy and overthinking what comes naturally. He is also prone to sinus problems, which are partially environmental/seasonal and which can thwart Aries's usual buoyancy. Like all the fire signs Aries rushes through these problems until they hamper his fun and enthusiasm. Then the idea of self-care becomes an immediate and necessary need. For any physical imbalances Aries may have, acupuncture can be a very good therapy—especially for headaches. The needles could be thought of as a "weapon" to reroute the energy traffic in Aries's system.

Psychological self-care for Aries is a bit more complex. Aries is just developing his personality. His naive and eternally youthful enthusiasm for life can appear abrupt. He doesn't think before he acts and this may make others angry. Aries is always stupefied when this happens because he doesn't really know what he did wrong. Conventional therapy usually is not effective for Aries because he is too busy getting on with life to contemplate the past or parse out why a relationship or event turned sour. His MO is to move on quickly and try again. Therapy apps may come in handy here, as well as talk therapy conducted over the phone. The exchange between therapist and client is often brief, but can be effective. This can help Aries sort out his energy and to improve his communication skills.

Aries and Self-Care Success

The pitfall for Aries's self-care program is any time things become too complicated. Aries needs a direct goal and a clear way to achieve it, otherwise he is likely to say, "I'm out of here!" Additionally, any activity that requires psychological subtlety with complex communication and emotions is a total downer for Aries. The sign is not superficial, but Aries is not interested in exploring shades of meaning. Rather, he operates in a direct line of action: I want to do this, so I do it. And if someone or something gets in the way, Aries either says that it isn't worth it or that tomorrow is another day.

Aries is at his best when pioneering new projects, and, when executed correctly, a self-care program can be an experience he relishes. His pursuit in taking care of himself is based on development of energy coordination, conservation of energy, and completion. This is his soul mission. When these goals align, he feels all the excitement of a child opening a gift—and there is no better gift than taking a vested interest in lifelong wellness. The best way to ensure wellness is by making self-care a priority in your life, so let's take a look at some self-care activities that are tailored specifically for you, Aries.

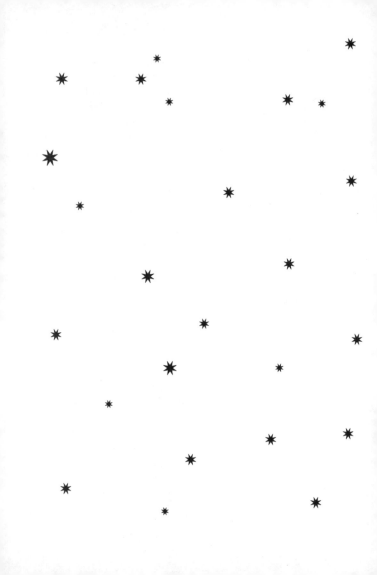

♈

PART 2

SELF-CARE
RITUALS
— FOR —
ARIES

Stargaze

The universe is expansive. Just look up at the sky on a pitch-black night. There are tiny suns and balls of flaming gas millions of miles away. Some estimates suggest there are approximately one hundred billion stars in just the Milky Way alone. Imagine how many more there are in the billions of other galaxies in the universe.

Your presence in this universe is important. Never lose the passion and heat you have burning inside you as a fire sign. It can be easy to feel small sometimes. When you are feeling lost, look up at the stars. They can help you find your way. And if you are lucky, you may even discover the constellations of one of the fire signs—Aries, Leo, or Sagittarius—to guide you.

Write Out Your Thoughts

Fire signs are known for following their gut instincts, but with all the background noise buzzing around you, it can be hard to hone in on what your gut is saying. Try a stream-of-consciousness writing exercise to amplify your inner monologue. First, clear your mind. Next, think about something you feel you need guidance on: anything from a career question, to relationships, to personal development. Then just start writing. Don't think too much about what you are writing; just allow the words to flow. Write for as long as you want. In the end you may find the answer you were looking for all along buried within your words.

Relax with a Bike Ride

As a fire sign, Aries thrives on heat and energy, so spending active time outside on a warm summer day is an ideal way to practice both physical and emotional self-care at the same time. Taking a relaxing bike ride is a great way to release the problems on your mind. Use the energy of the sun to recharge and reconnect with yourself. Clear your mind of all of the stress that's been following you and just focus on the road ahead, literally and metaphorically. But be careful! The head is ruled by Aries, so be sure to protect it with a sturdy helmet.

Sweat Your Way to Relaxation

While we often think of heat as linked to passion and intensity, it can also be incredibly restorative and relaxing for fire signs. Embrace the calming effect of heat by seeking out a sauna at your local gym or spa. Take time to lounge in the warmth, allowing the sweat to cleanse your body of impurities. Breathe in the heat and feel the heat soften your muscles and increase your circulation. As the warmth envelopes your body, any pain and stress will melt away.

Can't find a sauna nearby? No problem. Turn on your shower to hot and let the water run for a few minutes. Be sure to close your windows and bathroom doors. Then get a comfy seat and kick back in your own at-home sauna for some rest and recuperation.

Visit an Acupuncturist

Aries gets his energy from the head, so it makes sense that blocked sinuses could really slow you down. When pollen levels begin to rise, visit an acupuncturist to help clear your sinuses and relieve yourself of that stuffy, clogged feeling.

Acupuncture is a traditional Chinese medical practice that refocuses and realigns your chi (your natural life energy). Acupuncturists use thin needles placed at various pressure points around the body to put your chi back in its proper alignment and fix a variety of ailments. To drain sinuses, a skilled practitioner can use pressure points found around your nose and forehead to clear any blockages and help your energy flow once more. This will clear your head of the unnecessary pressure blocked sinuses can bring and give you your trademark energy back!

Clear Up Congestion

A stuffed or runny nose is miserable for anyone, but Aries is especially bothered since he is ruled by the head. When you're dealing with a head cold, it's time to slow down, rest, and drink plenty of fluids.

You might also find that a neti pot can help flush out your blocked nasal passages. A neti pot is a small teapot-like vessel that you fill with sterile water to make an irrigation solution. Stand over a sink and pour the solution into one nostril. The liquid should flow through your nasal passages and out the other nostril, clearing out mucus and freeing up the cilia that line your nasal cavities. (Be sure to follow the specific directions on your neti pot.) It might be just what you need to restore yourself to good health.

Practice Acrobatics for Flexibility

Aries is an intense sign who loves to burn up his excess energy with a heavy workout. But stiff, bulky muscles can lead to injuries, and Aries doesn't want to be slowed down. Get those muscles loose by practicing some acrobatics. The fluid movements and routines of acrobatics can stretch your muscles to attain greater flexibility and body control while helping to prevent injuries.

Find some beginners' classes near you to learn the basics before jumping in too far. Start off learning to do some handstands and slowly progress to backbends, tumbling, and maybe even some aerial arts! You'll find yourself getting a great full-body workout that uses your Aries energy to boost your flexibility and balance—while appealing to your sense of adventure.

Teach That Learning Is Power

It's as simple as ABC... As a fire sign, your ambition and passion for adventure has given you a lot of life experiences. Bring that passion and spirit you have for life to others by volunteering as a teacher in one capacity or another. This may mean becoming a mentor at a local after-school program, reading to children at the library, or teaching adults a special skill like painting or accounting at a community center. The choice is yours. But however you choose to go about it, know that instilling knowledge in others is an act of love and patience. A good teacher can inspire and motivate their students. And the benefit isn't just theirs. As a fire sign, engaging with a group can be incredibly fulfilling for you too. Take a survey of your many talents and see where you can help.

Flirt

Intimacy and sexual connection are key components in a relationship, especially for fire signs. You live to feel close to others and make your passion for them known in one way or another. When the mood strikes, unleash your inner flirt and have some fun with the person you are smitten with. Bat your eyes. Whisper sweet nothings. Tell them a corny joke. Let loose and show your unique personality.

Punch It Out!

A ries can be a determined sign and, like the Ram
that represents it, you may use this trait to push
your way to success in pretty much everything you
try. However, this level of intensity isn't always a good
thing for your health or overall well-being. Take care
of yourself by getting all that tension and intensity,
and any residual anger, out of your system...by taking
some swings at a punching bag!

Pretend you're punching that frustrating work
project, the coffee shop that never gets your order
right, or that computer that crashed right before you
were about to send your email. This type of physical
self-care will get your heart rate up—perfect for a fire
sign!—and you'll be able to clear your head and focus
on what's really important: you!

Take In a Sunset

The sun is very symbolic for fire signs. Its energy sustains and comforts you, so it's no surprise that watching the sun set after a long day can help you relax and find peace. Find a local spot with a great view if you can, and settle in for a show. Find solace in watching the different colors that emanate across the sky as the sun dips below the horizon: from bright orange, to light pink, soft periwinkle to, finally, a deep blue. Let the phases of its descent remind you that with every ending comes a beginning. The sun goes down, and the sun comes up.

Take a Road Trip

Satisfy your fiery sense of adventure with a spontaneous mini-road trip. Take the back roads, avoid
the highways, and make this a leisurely trip to clear
your mind, ease your spirit, and reignite your wander-
lust. You don't necessarily need to have a final destination in mind; just embrace the journey and the open
road. As you're driving, you can sing along to your
favorite playlist or put on a podcast or audiobook.
Take the time alone in your car to enjoy yourself and
your surroundings. It does not need to be a lengthy
drive in order to experience its benefits—you just need
to relax and enjoy the ride.

Enjoy a Laugh

When you're in need of emotional release, turn to your favorite laugh-out-loud comedy. It may seem counterintuitive, but a funny movie is actually one of the best ways a fire sign can let go of any nasty emotions that have been building up over time. You have so much passion swirling inside you that you need a positive way to let it all out. If you have a favorite comedy, turn it on—or if you want to try something new, check out what's playing at your local theater. Need more of a reason to laugh? Not only does laughter help reduce stress hormones in your body, it also helps increase immune cells and releases endorphins, the body's feel-good chemical. Win-win!

Make a List

———————

Fire signs often have a lot of great ideas and like to start a variety of projects when inspiration strikes. It's just part of the territory—you are naturally creative and dream big. The hurdle is completing these projects.

Take a survey of your life and make note of different projects or plans that are sitting around half-finished. Make a list of the tasks you want to complete and when you want to complete them by. You can be as specific or as vague as you want.

Maybe that wine rack you are building doesn't need to be finished for another year or so, or maybe you want to show off your favorite bottles by next month. The ultimate goal is committing to expectations and following through on your plans. And just imagine how much better you'll feel once you've checked off a few of those projects from your list.

Go for a Run

———————————

Aries is fueled by the power of Mars, which means you're an energetic go-getter. If you're feeling overwhelmed or stressed out, try heading out for a run. A slow jog probably won't do much for Aries— you'll want something fast-paced, because the more you sweat, the better you'll feel! To keep your runs from getting boring, create upbeat playlists, buy new workout clothes, and check out new trails periodically. Your Aries determination will love the challenge of a tough run, and you'll end up with a stronger body and a clearer mind.

Running is a great way to re-center yourself after a harried day—think of it as a meditative experience, and focus on your breathing and any beautiful scenery around you.

Become a Gamer

Fire signs are competitive when it comes to just about anything. Even the most mundane of tasks can become a game for you, one that you absolutely must win. To feed your competitive spirit in a healthy manner, try playing a board game. You're already used to being active outside, taking on one athletic challenge and then the next. Now train your mind. There are so many options to help you start flexing your brain muscles, from classic games like Monopoly and Scrabble to team games like charades, and even strategy and role-playing games. Buy a few and then have your friends over for a good old-fashioned game night!

Try Spontaneity

When is the last time you did something completely on impulse? Hopefully not too long ago, because enthusiastic spontaneity is the ruling philosophy for all fire signs. Have you been feeling a little trapped lately? Stuck in a rut you just can't break free from? Don't ignore that little voice inside you urging you to do something a little out of your comfort zone. Being impulsive and spontaneous ignites the fire sign's soul and feeds the energy within. Without it, you'll suffocate under the weight of predictability.

Burn, Baby, Burn

Fire is cathartic for fire signs. It can cleanse and purify your energy, and helps you let go of emotional burdens. From destruction comes regrowth, better and stronger than before.

Use the natural destruction inherent with fire to your advantage. Write down your feelings on a few pieces of paper. Light a candle and place it in a fire-safe bowl or in the sink. Carefully hold each piece of paper to the flame and allow it to catch fire. Watch as fire consumes your words and emotions. Drop the piece of paper into the sink or bowl to continue burning. As each emotion goes up in flames, feel the weight on your heart lessen. You are free, ready to rise from the ashes more resilient and determined.

Soak Up the Sun

It's time to turn up the heat! Fire signs need vacations just like everyone else, but when planning yours, stick to warm, sunny destinations. You need the heat to feed your soul. Ditch your coat and look for vacation spots on the beach, where the sun is strong and the temperatures soar. Fire signs are nourished by the heat, so soak up the rays for ultimate replenishment.

Keep your body and mind challenged with tons of adventures and new experiences. While taking some time to lounge and relax is totally fine, you need something to get your fire burning. Try to schedule at least one activity each day you are on vacation, whether that means going for a hike through canyons or learning to surf. The more out of your comfort zone you are, the more alive you'll feel.

Become More Patient

Fire signs have so many wonderful personality traits. Your level of loyalty, ambition, and passion is something to be envied. But you also have some unfavorable traits that you can work on. For example, your fieriness can often be interpreted by others as impatience. As a fire sign, your emotions tend to escalate very quickly, and your intensity can sometimes get the best of you.

Patience is a skill that often takes practice. Make it a personal goal to become more patient with others, situations, and yourself. When you feel that you are losing your patience, take a few deep breaths to de-escalate your emotions before they go too far. You have the power to control how you react to what you are feeling inside.

Find Your Passion

Discovering what kindles the passion inside you usually comes naturally for fire signs. After all you are full of strong emotions and big ideas, all of which drive your sense of knowing and well-being. Maybe it's a hobby that makes your heart sing, or a political cause, or a person. Hone in on those things and make them a prominent part of your life if they aren't already. Indulge in the passion you feel for them, and let it fill you with meaning and support. If you are unsure about what lights your fire, it's time to start learning about yourself. Try a new meal, make a new friend, read a new book. Your journey of self-discovery will lead you to your true passions.

Throw Darts to Relieve Stress

———————

Darts aren't just for dingy barrooms—they are a perfect game for Aries. Ruled by the war god Mars, Aries presides over sharp objects—and throwing darts is a great way to release any pent-up negative energy you have. Hang a dartboard on the back of your office door, in your garage, or in an outside space. You can find a dartboard to fit any aesthetic preference, from the traditional red and green style to a modern version with artwork on its face. As you get ready to play, take several deep breaths and re-cite a simple mantra like "This too shall pass" several times to quiet your mind. Then point your dart, and see how close you get to the bull's-eye!

Combine Earth and Fire

Stone is one of the earth's most sacred elements, and with a touch of heat, it becomes the ultimate healing tool. You can benefit from the combination of these two elements by indulging in a hot-stone massage.

Fire signs are naturally active beings, often pushing their bodies to the limit with exercise and adventure. Take time to let your body relax and heal after strenuous activity, and why not do so with a soothing hot-stone massage? Not only do the stones connect with the primal fire inside you, but they expand your blood vessels, improving circulation and flushing your skin, all while relaxing sore muscles.

Create a Good Sleep Routine

A good night's sleep can be transformative, but unfortunately, fire signs often have a hard time getting enough sleep. As a fire sign, you naturally need less sleep than others, but that doesn't mean you are invincible. It just means you have to work a little harder at giving yourself the best chance possible for restorative sleep.

Creating a good sleep routine is key. Do you already have a routine, or does it change from night to night? Do you have a specific bedtime you shoot for, or do you stay up until different times depending on your mood?

To help stabilize your sleep schedule, try implementing a few easy, enjoyable activities you can do right before bed, anything from reading for a few minutes to taking a long bath, or even meditating. Aim to get into bed at around the same time every night. Fire signs love spontaneity, but when it comes to good sleep hygiene, predictability is paramount.

Streamline Your Space

Clutter can do more than just cause a mess in your home. It can overwhelm your mind and make you feel trapped. Fire signs love big spaces with a lot of room to move around. If you find that you are feeling claustrophobic in your own living space, it might be time to streamline your belongings.

Start by going through your closets and cabinets and throw out anything you don't need. Next, move on to your furniture. Many fire signs find the minimalist design aesthetic a pleasing choice. Look for furniture that does double duty, like a combination desk and dining table. The most important thing is to give yourself space to feel free.

Don't Test Your Limits

Fire signs have a tendency to overexert themselves, physically and emotionally. Because of this it's important to recognize your limits, and to try not to push them too much. If you find you have a propensity for going too far emotionally, it might be time to create a list of warning signs that you can flag for yourself. When you see those warning signs popping up in your thought pattern and behavior, or if you feel yourself getting too stressed and overwhelmed, schedule a self-care activity to help find equilibrium once again. It can be as simple as taking a bath or visiting an old friend.

If you push yourself athletically, always give your body time to recuperate. While fire signs always want to go farther and be better physically, not allowing your body to rest after physical exertion can increase your risk for serious injury. Don't let your fire burn too bright—you are your own best advocate for balance and well-being.

Embrace H$_2$O

Water and fire are opposites. And while water can extinguish fire, those born as fire signs need water to keep them thriving and succeeding. With all the strenuous activities you do as a fire sign, don't forget to keep hydrated. It can be easy to forget to stop and drink water when you are focused on achieving a physical goal. Make it a priority to drink the recommended number of ounces of water a day, and more if you are engaging in demanding physical workouts. Remember that water will not smother the flame burning inside of you.

Tap Dance

If you're getting bored with your current exercise routine, try tapping! The percussive sounds of tap dancing are well suited to Aries's extroverted yang energy. If you're new to tap, don't worry—Aries's fearlessness and determination will ensure that you're brave enough to join a class and learn in no time. Many dance studios offer beginner adult classes in the evening, so grab a friend and pop into one. You'll work up a sweat dancing to the cheerful tunes and forget your worries at the same time. This invigorating dance style is also infectious and fun—you'll find your toes tapping even outside the class.

Beat the Heat

———————

Balance can be the key to a happy life. As a fire
sign, you must learn to offset your heat and
passion with coolness. Begin with how you nourish
your body. If it feels like your inner fire is burning too
hot, put away the spices and try to balance the heat
by eating cooling foods. Turn to foods such as water-
melon, cucumber, and yogurt, and if you are feeling
really indulgent, ice cream. The cool contrast will help
keep your inner fire from burning out of control.

Bang on the Bongos

Aries is represented by the Ram, and rams are known for butting things with their horns to get what they want. You may not have horns, but you do have hands—and you can use them to pound on a drum to change your mood and release stress.

Percussion instruments align well with Aries's outgoing, vibrant nature, and it's easy to get started playing simple drums like the bongos. Look for a class at a local arts center and lose yourself in that irresistible beat. Bongos can create many different types of music—so experiment with both energizing and upbeat options, and steady and relaxing ones.

Draw a Bath

As a fire sign, you already have a special affinity to heat and its galvanizing power. But it is also a wonderful relaxation tool. Warm water can be incredibly soothing for a weary fire sign. If your mind is cluttered from the demands of day-to-day life, and your muscles are sore from all of the physical activities you do, climb into a warm bath and let the water alleviate your ailments.

You can even add a special bath bomb or bubbles to the bath to make it more relaxing. Go for scents like lavender, jasmine, or even rose to ease your mind. Adding Epsom salt to the warm water can help take the ache out of overused muscles. Start by adding 1 cup of Epsom salt to the bath as the water runs.

Stand Up Tall

Even the most confident Aries can have moments of doubt. At those times your body language probably reflects your mood—you might be slouched, slumped, or hunched. Recharge yourself by taking a moment to focus on adjusting your posture. Stand up very straight and put your hands on your hips. Look straight ahead and take three slow, deep breaths. Sometimes acting as if you're confident can get your mind to believe it. This simple yet effective exercise has an amazing ability to reframe your mind-set, restore your self-confidence, and reclaim your leading Ram qualities!

Encourage Fireside Chats

The fireplace is often the center of the home. It's where people gather together to keep warm and to share stories. As a fire sign, you have an innate connection to fireplaces—they feel comfortable to you, like old friends. If you have a fireplace in your home, make it the center of your space. Arrange seating around the fireplace so it becomes the focal point. Use it as often as you can to take advantage of your sacred connection to the fire it contains.

If you don't have a fireplace already, you can often buy a decorative, portable fireplace from many home goods stores. Just the look of fire dancing can pacify a stressed-out fire sign. If you can't have any sort of fireplace, decorative or not, in your home, look for a restaurant or bar nearby that has one and make that your new go-to spot for drinks, dinner, and cozy relaxation.

Give Yourself Space to Think

Aries's busy mind and body are always working—but they need emotional and physical space to do their best work. Give yourself the physical freedom to thrive by walking around your home or office while you think. Pacing keeps your body busy, and Aries loves thinking in motion. See if your furniture could be pushed against the wall to open up some space. If your home or office doesn't have the space you need, take a break and move around outside. You will find yourself more relaxed and more productive as a result.

Find the Perfect Winter Hat

Because Aries rules the head, it's very important for you to take good care of yours. That's why hats are a great idea for Aries—preferably red ones, since it's Aries's signature color and reminiscent of your fiery personality. When it's cold out, remember that you can lose up to 10 percent of your body heat through your head. Invest in a breathable and warm hat to keep your head and ears toasty and comfortable no matter how bitter the cold.

Treat Yourself

You spend a lot of time entertaining those around you. The energy you have as a fire sign is infectious, so it's no wonder that people are drawn to you. You also love making people smile and laugh—it comes naturally and boosts your mood. Despite your penchant for entertaining, it's important to give yourself a break every once in a while. Alone time can be just as beneficial as time spent with large groups. Take yourself out to dinner once a month as a treat. To keep things lively, sit at the bar and people watch. Keep yourself open to new conversation with other bar patrons. Allowing your server to wait on you for once will help rejuvenate your spirit.

Get Creative

Being creative comes naturally to fire signs. They are often temperamental and passionate, and need a healthy way to release the emotions inside of them. While many fire signs turn to physical activities like athletics to help control the blaze within, flexing your creative muscles can be just as beneficial. Try indulging in the creative arts as inspiration. Hobbies such as painting, pottery, coloring, writing, or even knitting or scrapbooking can fuel your creative spark. Get a friend to join you as well. There are tons of ways to let your creativity run free. The only limit is your own imagination.

Take a Trip

Fire signs are drawn to impulse and improvisation. If they don't feed their desire for adventure on a regular basis, fire signs can sometimes get cranky and start feeling stuck. To remedy this, cash in your airplane miles and take a last-minute trip to somewhere you've always wanted to visit. Even a last-minute weekend trip to another town nearby can satisfy a fire sign's need for fresh scenery. Your need to explore unfamiliar territory can lead you to great discoveries about yourself and the world around you. Don't let the fear of the unknown stop you. Be spontaneous!

Greet the Day

Whether you are an early bird or a night owl, as a fire sign you have a natural attraction to the sun. You are drawn to its power and heat, and can often generate strength from its rays. Don't ignore this special connection you have with the sun. Embrace its energy and start your day by going for a long morning walk. Beginning the day by communing with the element that speaks to you the most will help set the stage for a positive afternoon, evening, and night ahead.

Check In on Your Emotions

Your emotional health is often overlooked when you're a fire sign. You are constantly moving from one thing to the next, so you may not make time to take your emotional temperature. Fire signs also spend a lot of time supporting and entertaining others emotionally. You are the first to step up and help a friend in need, but that concern doesn't transfer to your own well-being. Check in with yourself as often as possible. Are you stressed? Tired? Overwhelmed? Make a list of what you are feeling. If any of those feelings intensify, take some time to practice self-care in whatever form that suits you best.

Wear Fun Baseball Caps

Everyone should protect themselves from the sun's rays with hats—but it's especially important for Aries, who rules the head. This self-care act can do wonders for your skin health. Instead of straw hats, try fun baseball hats instead! They're more likely to match your energetic personality. Though red is Aries's signature color, you can experiment with any colors or styles to match your preferences. You can also look for hats with words or phrases that align with your passions and interests. If typical baseball hats tend to make your head too hot, look for breathable, moisture-wicking fabrics.

Clear Out Stale Energy with Sage

_____

Sometimes energy can linger, even after a person or influence has left a space. If someone left positive energy in your home, that's great! But if the energy that remains is negative or stale, it's time to cleanse the space and restore positive energy to your home. Burning sage is a time-honored Native American practice that clears energy—and it's simple and easy to do.

First, purchase some ceremonial sage (not the type found in the spice aisle at grocery stores). Second, tidy up any obvious clutter and open as many doors and windows as possible in your home. Finally, place the sage in a fireproof bowl and light it. Blow it out and use your hands to direct the smoke around your home. Both your body and your home will feel more open, more relaxed, and more balanced.

Just Say No

Fire signs are prone to saying yes to everything, almost to a fault. You tend to move from one activity to the next, accepting the latest invite and helping friends whenever they need. That's wonderful for everyone else, but it also means you burn both ends of your candle, until sometimes the only thing left is ashes. To help keep your fire from going out, practice saying no when you are feeling overextended. This may happen at work, with friends, with your family, or even to yourself. Prioritize your own needs over others. Know there is nothing wrong with taking time to stoke your own flame.

Go on a Social Media Detox

Fire signs love to live in the moment, but don't ruin that moment by feeling the need to update your social media accounts. By taking a step back from your online presence, you allow yourself to be present and fully experience the world around you. Rather than fearing missing out on the things you see people post about, go out into the world and enjoy them yourself.

Social media can be a great way to stay in touch with friends and family; however, don't let it be the only way you communicate and tend to your relationships. A social media detox allows you to rekindle these connections and share your stories in person.

Feng Shui Your Bed Placement

According to the Chinese art of feng shui, the placement of your bed can impact your health and well-being. You likely spend a good chunk of your 24-hour day in bed, so you might as well make the most of it.

Set up your bed so that your head faces east and your feet west as you sleep. If it's comfortable for you, sleeping toward the east is the most beneficial direction for Aries. If you have a window in the east, the rays of the rising sun can gently wake you in the morning, ensuring a relaxing and calm start to your day.

Delight in a Deep-Tissue Massage

Do your sore muscles need a little TLC? Soothing touch is a great way to alleviate stress in your body and your mind. As a fire sign, ignite a different type of heat inside you by turning to the therapeutic benefits of deep-tissue massage. The warmth created by kneading muscle tissue and improved blood circulation can ease chronic tension, pain, and stiffness. And this deeply therapeutic ritual can help calm anxiety and worry as well.

Place your trust in an experienced massage therapist. Before your massage starts, tell them exactly how your body feels and what it needs to get better. Keep in mind that a deep-tissue massage should never be painful, so don't be afraid to speak up at any point during your massage. Communication is key.

Strike a Work-Life Balance

As a fire sign, you have a passion to succeed in every aspect of your life. While this burning desire to achieve greatness powers your professional performance, it can also cause your work life to take over your whole life. It's important for your overall well-being that you keep your life inside the office balanced with your life outside the office. If you set boundaries between your professional and personal lives, you will be more productive at work and more fulfilled outside of it. You don't want to neglect your work responsibilities, but it's important to disconnect and recharge. By striking this work-life balance, you'll continue to succeed without burning out.

Get Some Fresh Air

Oxygen feeds fire, so when you feel your spark starting to dim, take 10 minutes to go outside and breathe in the fresh air. Whether you're at work or at home, it's the perfect way to take some time for yourself and recharge. As you're enjoying the fresh air, allow yourself to live in that moment. Take a deep, meaningful breath in through your nose, hold for 5 seconds, and breathe out through your mouth. Feel the air fill your lungs and circulate through your body. This simple mindful breathing exercise feeds your internal flame, calms your mind, and reenergizes your spirit.

Forgive Yourself

As a fire sign, it's easy to go from passionate to incensed. Usually, these feelings are reserved for people who aren't able to keep up with your fiery spirit. However, what happens when you are the one you're upset with? If you've done something that's created your own mental hang-up, you need to extinguish those feelings sooner rather than later. You don't want to be your own worst enemy. While it's important to keep yourself accountable, you also need to be able to forgive yourself for any missteps or mistakes you've made. Release those feelings that have been burning you up inside and channel your energy into positive thoughts and actions.

Don't Skimp on the SPF

Just because fire signs have a unique connection to the sun doesn't mean they still can't get burned by its power. Given the amount of time you spend outside keeping active, make sure to wear sunscreen and/or protect your skin with UV-blocking clothing. Hats are particularly important, as is reapplying sunscreen every hour or so when you are in the sun. If you've already spent too much time outside and gotten burned, a bottle of aloe vera gel can soothe the sting and help your skin heal more quickly.

Make 'Em Laugh

There's nothing quite like the power of a good belly laugh. Fire signs are extroverts by nature and love to entertain people with stories, songs, and even jokes. While you may not have an entire stand-up comedy set ready to go yet, all it takes is one simple joke to get someone laughing and improve their day. And that rush of joy coursing through your veins as your audience laughs is enough to raise any fire sign's temperature. Don't know any good jokes off the top of your head? Go for the classics or search online for some new material. And remember, it's all in the delivery!

Protect Your Energy While You Sleep

_____

You may not think much about what direction your feet are pointing while you sleep. But if they're pointed directly at a door, you can lose energy while you sleep, according to the Chinese art of feng shui. Doors can pull energy away from a sleeping person, and sleeping with your feet toward one can leave you feeling drained and tired in the morning.

Instead, try to position your bed or your feet so they're not facing a door—a wall is a much better option. You'll wake up refreshed, restored, and ready to take on the day.

Spice It Up!

Aries is passionate, adventurous, and energetic—and your diet should reflect those traits. To make sure that it does, nourish your body and mind with a range of healthy whole foods seasoned with various spices. Avoid falling into a rut by changing up spice choices and combinations frequently. Whether you pair classics like garlic and basil or rosemary and thyme, or branch out and create a new mixture all your own, your taste buds will thank you. Try out various spice combinations on the vegetables and proteins in your diet for meals that satisfy and energize you.

Burn Up the Competition

————————

Fire signs thrive off of a little friendly competition—the key word being friendly! Engage your fiery competitive side in a healthy way by joining a community sports league of your choosing. You may find that team sports, like soccer, kickball, basketball, volleyball, or even a running group, suit you best. The sense of comradery can jump-start that passion inside you for action. Use the energy and excitement coming from your teammates as fuel. Just remember, it's only a game. No matter if your team wins or loses, the primary goal is to have fun and get your body moving.

Inspire Others

———————

You are lucky to have such a powerful flame burning inside you. Fire signs may forget that not everyone possesses their same ambition and fervor. Use your natural fire for good and inspire someone else in your life.

Try sending a friend or a loved one a card of encouragement. The small gesture can help light a fire under them and give them the strength to take a risk. If sending a card isn't your cup of tea, a text, email, or phone call can offer the same sentiment. The goal is to reach out and share your own fire with someone else who needs it.

Use Iron Cookware

Mars, which rules Aries, is aligned with metals like iron, so it makes sense that you would benefit from using iron pans when you cook. Their durability, versatility, and high-quality makeup means that they're a practical choice as well. After you season a cast-iron skillet, it becomes nonstick, and is perfect for sautéing the spicy mixtures that Aries likes. Cast-iron pans also transfer seamlessly from stove top to oven, so they can accommodate a wide range of recipes. Sauté your favorite protein in a fiery spice combination in your cast-iron pan, and you'll be a believer in no time.

Savor Saffron in Your Dishes

Sharp and tangy saffron is a wonderful spice for the fiery Aries. Saffron comes from crocuses, the first flowers of spring, and is therefore associated with Aries's season as well.

This spice pairs well with such varied foods as apples, lamb, seafood, and citrus fruits, and is known for being a foundational flavor in classic paella (which you can make in an Aries-friendly cast-iron pan!) and risotto dishes. Saffron is expensive, but treating yourself to it once in a while is a worthy indulgence. Slow down and savor the exquisite flavors as you enjoy your meal.

Try Horseradish for a Condiment

The old standbys of ketchup and mustard aren't always flavorful enough for Aries's fire-seeking taste buds. Mix things up and try horseradish on fish, salads, and meats.

Horseradish is actually a root vegetable that, when grated, exudes a strong mustardy odor from the oils inside it. This strong flavor can clear out your sinuses, which are ruled by Aries. You can make a basic horseradish sauce at home by peeling and grating fresh horseradish root and combining it with vinegar, or mix the grated root with prepared mustard, mayonnaise, or cocktail sauce to spice up those condiments.

Let It Go

_____

Holding on to negative emotions can do long-term damage to your well-being. Because of how passionate you can be as a fire sign, you may find you let resentment or other destructive feelings boil inside you. Let those feelings go. Don't allow them to fester and build inside of you until they get to an unmanageable point. Release any grudges you have against a person who has wronged you and forgive them for their wrongdoing. Once you let these emotions loose into the universe, you'll begin to heal and open up to more positivity and light.

Enlist in Boot Camp

Boot camp–style exercise classes are popular
fitness options for fire signs looking to add a
little heat to their typical workout regime. These boot
camps attract a wide variety of people, and the group
atmosphere can really ignite a spark for fire signs
who love a little friendly competition. You'll learn to
encourage others to push their physical limit, and
to push your own limit as well. The combination of
intense cardiovascular or strength-training exercises
with a supportive team dynamic can be a rewarding
experience for many fire signs. Make friends, build
muscle, and tone your heart, all at the same time.

Seek Your Fire Totem

Your fire is unique to you. To remind yourself of this, seek out a personal totem that symbolizes your fire and flame that you can keep with you at all times. A totem is a sacred object that serves as an emblem for a group of people. In your case this totem will symbolize your connection to the fire burning within. It could be a piece of jewelry such as a bracelet, necklace, cuff, or amulet, or even a small desk trinket that you can keep by your side at work. There's no right or wrong when it comes to choosing your totem. Focus on something that calls to you and makes you feel brave and powerful when it is in your presence.

Take a Risk

You already know that, as a fire sign, you have great instincts, but you may struggle with acting on them. Trust your gut and take a risk. Ask someone out on a date, apply for a new job, or make a large purchase that you've been eyeing for a while. Do something risky for yourself. It's easy to tell yourself "I'll do it later" or "It's not the right time." There's no time like the present. It might seem scary when you are in the moment, but big risks often mean big rewards. Tap into that passion churning inside you and take a leap of faith.

Refresh Yourself with a Watercress Salad

A midday salad can do wonders for your body and mind—it's a light meal that keeps you fueled but doesn't weigh you down. But boring iceberg lettuce can get old quickly for Aries. Instead, try a dark, leafy green watercress salad—its peppery flavors suit Aries's fiery tastes. Plus, it packs a powerful nutritional punch—watercress contains lots of vitamin K (which helps with bone health and blood clotting) and vitamin A (which supports skin health, boosts immunity, and improves vision) and is also a source of calcium, manganese, and potassium. Eat the salad slowly and mindfully so you can relish the intense flavors you're experiencing.

Make a Game of It

_____

Fire signs can get bored easily. They are drawn to adventure and spontaneity, so the last thing they want is to get stuck in a pattern of tedium. Unfortunately, everyone has responsibilities they would rather not do, but how you react to those responsibilities is your choice. Tap into your fun-loving nature and make things more playful. Whether it's at work or around the house, turn your chores and responsibilities into a game. Even something as mundane as vacuuming the living room becomes a game when you set a timer for yourself. It makes things fun, feeds your competitive nature, and gets finished what needs to be done. In the end, changing how you think about a task can change how you complete it.

Smile

Smiling can change how you see the world, and how the world sees you. In fact some studies suggest that the physical act of smiling can trick your brain into being happy even when you are in a bad mood. As a fire sign, you have so much love and happiness inside you—let it shine through and catch on like wildfire. Make a deal with yourself to smile at one stranger a day. Because your happy energy is contagious as a fire sign, this small act of kindness could do wonders for boosting someone's mood.

Spark Your Creativity
with a Fire Craft

Fuel your creative spark by taking up a craft that is powered by fire. While regular crafting such as painting, drawing, and sculpting are all wonderful ways to unwind and explore your artistic side, as a fire sign you crave something with a little more heat. Try pottery making, glassblowing, or woodburning to satiate your appetite. Your innate connection to fire will only deepen your creative reach and encourage your imagination. Find inspiration in how the heat transforms different materials—how it hardens clay, melts glass, and singes wood. Honor the power of fire through the creative process.

Visit a Thai Restaurant

If your fridge is empty and you've had a busy week, it's time to relax and let someone else do the cooking. Consider heading out to a local Thai place once a month for a fragrant and filling meal.

Thai food in particular is great for Aries's passion for boldness, so grab a friend and indulge in a meal that appeals to all of your senses. You'll find your Aries enthusiasm fired up with the intensely delicious flavors of dried chilies, coriander, ginger, star anise, and even sriracha. Choose your favorite classic dish, or try one of the restaurant's new options for a contemporary twist.

Create a Sanctuary for Sleep

If you often have trouble falling asleep or staying asleep, you might want to examine the mirrors in your bedroom. The Chinese art of feng shui teaches that mirrors can make anxiety worse, and can bounce energy around a room in a frenetic way. Unfortunate mirror placement in a bedroom can therefore lead to an unpleasant sleeping environment.

To be sure your mirrors aren't causing stress or sleeplessness, do not place mirrors so they are facing your bed. You shouldn't be able to see your reflection in a mirror while lying in bed.

Turn Up the Heat

_____

Who says those veggies have to be bland and boring? Add some zip to your food by adding some red pepper flakes to your dishes. Aries enjoys spice and excitement, and even a little burst of it with your food can do wonders. The fire in the flavor will be sure to satisfy Aries's appetite and keep him eating right.

This type of self-care can help improve your mood and give you extra energy exactly when you need it. While it's important to eat healthy, balanced meals, you can still add extra fun to your day with some heat at just the right time. Kick the spice up a notch with your cooking to ensure a delightful and delectable feast.

Binge a New Show

There's nothing quite like snuggling up on the couch in front of your TV (or laptop) after a long day. As a fire sign, you've probably been jumping from one activity to the next, trying to keep active and keep yourself moving. But there's nothing wrong with slowing down for a bit. Binge-watching a new show can be the perfect break you need from your hectic schedule. Make a night of it, and burn through every episode you can find. Make a bowl of popcorn, open a bottle of wine, and kick off your shoes. Let yourself become obsessed with knowing what happens next.

Boost Your Immune System with Garlic

Your immune system is responsible for keeping all of your body's systems functioning at their best, so it's important to take good care it. You can do that by getting plenty of rest, eating a healthy diet of whole foods, and drinking lots of water. You can also turn to an ingredient that has been proven to increase the number of T cells (which fight off disease) in your blood and help you recover from colds faster: garlic. Garlic is also associated with the planet Mars, which rules Aries, so it's an especially good fit for the Ram.

Garlic is a very versatile seasoning—it pairs well with many different foods, and you can make its flavor sharper or more mellow depending on your personal preference. (If you're worried about your breath, just chew a little parsley after you eat!)

Start an Idea Book

Fire signs are known for their creativity and great ideas. Don't risk letting those good ideas slip away by not taking the time to write them down. Consider buying an idea journal where you can keep track of all the cool things that you come up with on a daily basis. Similar to a dream journal, an idea journal is the perfect place to house your million-dollar thoughts. These journals are specifically created to help you tease out and capture your next great idea, and many even have prompts to inspire and challenge you. Never forget another genius idea again!

Fight for Your Rights

———————

Use your passion to change the world. Fire signs have a lot of strong opinions and personal beliefs. Identify those causes that mean the most to you and put all of your energy into fighting for them. Whether it's environmental issues, animal welfare, women's and LGBTQ+ rights, veterans' affairs, or anything else that lights your fire, know that you can make a difference just by showing up and being present. Start by joining a social media group that gives updates about organized protests near you. Volunteer on weekends at local shelters. Make signs for rallies. Whatever it takes. Fight for what you believe, and inspire and motivate others to do the same.

Make Your Own Rose Mist

Self-care may not come easy to a fire sign. You are used to caring for others, and can sometimes forget to tend your own fire. Before you know it, your flame is burning out of control. A refreshing mist is a quick and easy way to balance the fire inside you.

Rosewater is especially therapeutic for irritated skin. Rosewater is a hydrating blend made by steeping rose petals in water. Spritz it over clean skin and breathe in the calming scent of roses. Take a moment to pause and enjoy the sensations around you.

While you can find rosewater in many grocery and health stores, you can also make your own. First, boil a large pot of water, and remove the petals from a few roses. Add the petals to the water, and allow to simmer over medium-high heat for 20–30 minutes, or until the petals have lost the majority of their color. Cool, strain the petals, and add the water to a clean spray bottle.

Sip Ginger Tea

Even high-energy Aries needs to relax sometimes! Make your moments of relaxation delicious by sipping on some restorative ginger tea as you recharge and reboot. This hot-blooded fire sign typically loves spice, both in his food and in his life, and the subtle heat of the ginger will help keep Aries warm, well-rested, and rejuvenated.

Try making homemade ginger tea: simply peel and slice a 2-inch section of fresh ginger, and then boil the slices in 1½ to 2 cups of water for 10 minutes (for a milder tea) to 20 minutes (for stronger tea). Use the time while the water is boiling to meditate or visualize yourself in a peaceful scene. Remove from heat, strain to remove the ginger, and add honey if desired.

Decorate Your Home with Chinese Ginger Jars

Ginger is a powerful spice that matches Aries's passion for intense flavors. Try storing ginger in a ginger jar and protect your spice while adding beautiful décor to your home. Chinese ginger jars are painted with elaborate and intricate designs (often in the color blue, but available in other colors too) such as flowers, dragons, and landscapes. The jars vary in size but usually have rounded tops and small openings. They make a visually interesting addition to any kitchen shelf. They're so beautiful that you might find yourself building a small collection!

Have a Solo Dance Party

Break out your dancing shoes and turn on your favorite jam. It's time for a solo dance party! Dancing is a wonderful way for fire signs to expel built-up energy that they haven't been able to let go of yet. It gets your heart pumping and your endorphins flowing. Plus, it's just plain fun. Let loose and really go for it. There's no one there to judge your dance moves or the song you pick to boogie down to. Let the music take control and just go with it. Feel like doing the electric slide? Do it. Want to practice your running man? There's no time like the present!

Take Your Vitamins

_____

Your body is a temple, and it needs the proper nourishment to stay strong and healthy. Fire signs are constantly pushing their physical limits by taking on new athletic challenges. To keep your body from getting run-down, it's important to stick to a vitamin regimen every day. Talk to your doctor about which vitamins are best for you. There are even companies that offer personalized vitamin packs based on your individual needs. Even just a simple multivitamin made for your age group or gender can give your body the boost it needs.

Relax with Incense

After a long, busy day, it can be hard for the energetic Aries to unwind. If you're feeling restless and your mind is racing, try to quiet it with some deep breathing while you enjoy incense burning. Choose any type of incense you like, but look for an incense burner made of tiger's eye or malachite. Both of these stones are associated with Aries and are very compatible with Aries's personality.

As you breathe in the smell of the incense, gaze at the stone burners and reap the additional self-care benefits: the deep brown and orange tiger's eye is known to help concentration and decrease anxiety, and it's associated with the health of the nose, which is ruled by Aries. Malachite's stunning green swirls help you push out of everyday sadness and find new growth and progress.

Soothe Sore Muscles
with Arnica

A ries likes to put his all into everything he does. Whether it's a morning run, a work project, or a volunteer position, Aries gives 100 percent all the time. All that dedication can lead to sore muscles once in a while—legs that burn from a run, tense shoulders and neck from a long day at the office, or a sore back from an afternoon of hard work. That soreness is your body telling you to slow down and heal. Try rubbing arnica cream or gel (which comes from a yellow daisy-like flower) into your muscles and joints; it comes in cream or gel forms. Arnica can stimulate circulation and decrease inflammation, thus relieving your pain.

Avoid Burnout

With all the complicated emotions you hold onto as a fire sign, it can sometimes be helpful to seek out a professional therapist to work through your thoughts. Talking to a professional is often a therapeutic experience and can promote overall wellness in your life. Fire signs are prone to emotional fatigue and burnout because their emotions run intensely for extended periods of time. It can drain your system to keep them bottled up. Eventually, you'll run out of gas. Turning to a trained professional who can help you understand and sort your stressors can save your emotional well-being and give you a healthy outlet to better yourself.

Change It Up

Predictability is the fire sign's ultimate enemy. How do you avoid getting stuck in the same humdrum pattern? Change things up. Start in your home, where you spend the majority of your time and where you feel the most comfortable.

To get the winds of change blowing, open your windows (if you can) and move your furniture around into different arrangements in all of your major spaces. This could mean moving your bed from one wall to the other or changing which direction your couch faces. It could also mean doing something as small as adding a piece of furniture to a room. Whatever feels right to you! Sometimes just changing your perspective can make all the difference in the world.

Treat Yourself to a Cardamom Coffee

A morning cup of coffee is almost a ritual unto itself: a quiet kitchen, a beautiful mug, the mesmerizing swirl of the steam. Kick your morning cup up a notch by adding a small amount of cardamom to your coffee. This spice, used frequently in Middle Eastern cooking, is an Aries favorite because of its bold herbal and piquant flavors. High-quality cardamom is expensive, so only indulge once in a while in small amounts. Savor the unique combination of coffee and cardamom as you contemplate your day.

Host a Henna Party

Perhaps one of the most effective types of self-care is to relax and talk with good friends. There's just no substitute for casual, meandering conversations, abundant laughter, and heartfelt, genuine connections. The next time your group gets together, consider making it a henna party.

Henna is a natural reddish-brown plant dye that you can paint on your skin to create temporary body art (henna should not be black or contain any unsafe added chemicals). In the Middle East (an Aries-ruled area), people often celebrate gatherings by painting amazingly intricate designs on their face and hands with henna. If you've never created henna patterns before, search online for how-to instructions and add a new dimension to your nights in with friends.

Boost Productivity
with a Mirror

Aries loves to be in command. Watching himself taking charge is a very effective way to maintain self-confidence and boost productivity. Try hanging a mirror in front of your desk, at home or at work, so you can see your whole face and head. The power of watching yourself thrive while you work does wonders for your emotional health—don't be surprised if you start coming up with even more amazing ideas than before. Plus, no one can sneak up on you!

Try the Ancient Power
of Hot Yoga

Bikram yoga is a form of yoga done in an environ-ment where the temperature is about 104°F. Heat is a vital element of this exercise. Practicing yoga in a heated room is a great way to potentially increase your metabolism and your heart rate, which in turn allows your blood vessels to expand and your muscles to become more flexible.

This form of hot yoga is perfect for fire signs. Fire signs feed off of the heat around them, and use it to find equilibrium and balance. Look for hot yoga classes near you to challenge yourself and your body. If you've never tried a hot yoga class before, be sure to hydrate your body beforehand and to bring a small towel with you to class. Get ready to sweat!

Follow Your Intuition

Your intuition is invaluable when it comes to decision-making. Fire signs often move from one idea to the next rather quickly, but your gut reaction to an idea can help inform whether you should pursue it or not. You don't have the time to sit and weigh the pros and cons, using your mind to decide. You use your heart and that feeling pulsing inside either urging you forward or calling out warnings to stop. Listen to that voice. It tells the most primal truths about your journey as a person, and its only purpose is to help you navigate through life's confusing moments.

Still aren't sure what your intuition is telling you? Sometimes, it can even be a physical feeling. Do you get a warm rush in your veins when you think of something? Or is it more of a stomachache? Our bodies have different ways of speaking to us. Listen for yours.

Clear Your Desk,
Clear Your Mind

Because Aries is such a hard worker, you probably take on many tasks in your job or at home. That strategy can be rewarding—but it can also be overwhelming. One technique that can help you manage a heavy workload is to clear off your work space as best you can every night. If paperwork and clutter begin to pile up, it can give Aries the impression that he'll never finish it all—and that self-doubt won't sit well with such a focused and determined personality. The same cleanup approach works for your inbox—try to file or delete as much digital clutter as you can every night so you can start fresh and motivated the next morning.

Decorate Your Desk with a Single Flower

Being stuck inside all day working can wear down the adventurous Aries. Bring a little bit of nature inside by placing a single flower in a vase on your desk. Because red is your natural color, look for a red bird-of-paradise, gerbera daisy, or poppy. Not only are these stunning flower choices visually interesting, but they'll also keep you upbeat and energetic as you go through your workday. When the color or petals begin to fade, replace the flower with a new one.

Rest Easy with Green Malachite

Green malachite is associated with Aries, and it's a gorgeous stone with many amazing properties. While toxic in its unfinished state, when polished and finished, it is commonly used in the creation of figurines or jewelry. Malachite is a protective stone that can cleanse your energy and the energy of the space it's in. It's also a stone that can bring with it good fortune and wealth. Green malachite is especially useful near your bed because it can stimulate positive dreams and bring vivid memories to life. Restful sleep is a vital part of self-care, and sleeping next to green malachite will ensure that you wake up restored and refreshed.

Add a Splash of Color and Sound with a Cinnabar Bracelet

Your signature color of bold red lends itself well to accents in your wardrobe. Try out cinnabar bracelets (for men and women) for a distinctive and multisensory option. Traditional cinnabar bracelets were made with a red mineral that contained mercury. Nowadays, they're made with lacquered wood and carved with intricate designs. When you wear two or more together, they click and clack against each other, making a light percussive sound that's appealing to Aries. Wearing them will make you feel dynamic, confident, and unique!

Catch Some Rays

_____

Spending time outside soaking up the sun can lift any fire sign's mood. Think of yourself as a solar panel. You need the sunlight to reenergize your soul when you are feeling depleted. Lucky for fire signs, sunlight can help increase your levels of serotonin—those feel-good chemicals in your brain—thus boosting your happy mood.

Take some time to bathe in the sun, letting the rays wash over you. Feel the warmth on your skin, and imagine the sunshine penetrating down into your heart, lighting you up on the inside. Bask in the warmth around you.

While sun exposure, at the right times and intensity, can be beneficial for anyone, too much sun can be dangerous, even if you are a fire sign. While you're recharging in the sun, always take the proper precautions, like wearing sunscreen and remembering to reapply.

Let's Get Physical

Making time for yourself can be difficult when you are a fire sign. You are always going, going, going, with very little downtime. There's always so much to do, and so little time to do it. Who wants to spend their free time going to the doctor? But, as a fire sign, it's important to make your health a priority. You tend to push yourself both physically and mentally, striving for the next success benchmark. Make sure you keep tabs on your health, and schedule an annual physical checkup with your doctor to make sure you are healthy and strong. Your wellness should never be put on the back burner.

Use Bergamot Oil to Fall Asleep Fast

If you tend to toss and turn before you fall asleep, it may be time to re-evaluate your bedtime routine. If you are typically looking at a screen right before trying to sleep, you're inadvertently stimulating your mind, not quieting it. Instead, try meditating, reading a book, or writing in a journal for several minutes before you shut off the light. Another tactic that's especially effective for Aries is putting a few drops of bergamot oil on your pillow before you go to bed (diluted according to instructions). Bergamot is the oil in Earl Grey tea and is aligned with Aries. Its relaxing and calming qualities will help prepare you for a night of peaceful rest.

Re-Center Yourself
with Patchouli

———————————

Aries's active mind and body can be hard to slow down. But sometimes taking a few quiet moments to recharge will help you be more productive and energetic going forward. Aromatherapy is a great resource for re-centering because it encourages you to slow down and breathe deeply.

Try applying some patchouli scent to your temples when you need to find balance. The strong, musky scent is a good match for Aries's assertive personality. Take several deep breaths and relax while you massage the oil (diluted according to instructions) into your temples. Then get ready to take on whatever task awaits you.

Escape to the Desert

Some people might think of clear waters and white sand when they think of vacations, but Aries might also want to consider another destination. The wide sky and intense heat of the desert is a perfect match for Aries's fiery personality. The expansiveness of the desert is also a reminder of the infinite possibilities of the world—and a motivation for Aries to find his place in it. There are many amazing desert resorts around the world where you can enjoy the luxuries you expect on a vacation *and* find the peace of miles of uninterrupted sand.

If you can't get away just yet, instead just visualize a desert scene to relax yourself. Imagine feeling the hot sun on your skin, seeing the beautiful patterns in the sand, and hearing the wind as it whistles over dunes.

Discover Florence

Travel—whether in person or through pictures or videos—is a great way to recharge yourself. The Aries-ruled Italian city of Florence is an especially amazing destination. Its unparalleled architecture, delicious food, and hospitable people are undoubtedly worth a trip overseas. Florence sits in the popular region of Tuscany, which is well known for its gorgeous vistas and incomparable wineries.

If you can't make it in person, instead explore the city via books full of photographs, interactive websites that teach you about its history, or food or travel shows that visit this unique spot. Just looking at images will enable you to relax and imagine that you're sitting at a café in central Florence, watching the bustle of people, listening to the chime of the Duomo's church bells, and sipping a cup of *caffè*.

Keep Your Cool

Fire signs can be temperamental at times. It's not your fault. You are naturally feisty and passionate, both positive traits that make you loyal and hard-working. Sometimes, though, you can get a little too overheated. At that point it's important to take a step back before you lose your cool too much. One trick you can try is to count to five in your head, or out loud. An alternate option is to exhale first and then inhale and repeat three times. Either way, you'll give yourself a moment to curtail the strong emotions that are driving you. Practice tamping down the fire within you without letting it go out.

Go on a Digital Detox

Fire signs are always moving from one thing to the next. That's because they are ambitious and motivated, traits that can sometimes lead to some serious burnout if you aren't careful.

One way to purposefully give yourself a break from the fast pace of the world around you is to unplug digitally as often as possible. Try and put your phone or tablet away at the same time every night, approximately an hour before bedtime. This gives your mind time to unwind before sleep.

If you go on vacation, consider switching your phone on just once a day to check for urgent messages. At home, designate a basket for devices and ask that family members place their phones and tablets in it before time meant to be spent together. And when going to dinner with friends, focus on enjoying your food and company—not keeping one eye on your phone at all times.

Watch a Circus

Circuses aren't just for kids anymore! Modern circus events encompass much more than clowns—you can find talented acrobats, lively music, and magical stories.

When you need to relax at a fun event, consider getting tickets to a circus. You're sure to see some fire-based tricks—right up Aries's alley—and will be treated to sights and sounds you won't see anywhere else. Whether you opt for a traditional type of circus outside under a tent or see a Cirque du Soleil show in a theater, the unique entertainment will help you laugh and forget all your worries.

Get Enough Rest

———————

Aries is always going, going, going. This lifestyle leads to so much success and fulfillment, but it can also lead to exhaustion if you're not mindful. Because Aries isn't naturally one to slow down and rest, you'll have to remind yourself to do that every once in a while.

Listen to the signs that your body needs to recharge—are you achy and yawning, or run down and restless? Take a mental health day off work, visit a calming outdoor location, and sit on a blanket under a tree. Read, nap, or just look at the clouds moving past. This type of self-care is just as important as eating vegetables or getting exercise, so be sure to prioritize it in your schedule.

Try an Extreme Sport

Aries is an adventurous, daring spirit. Feed your thirst for excitement by trying an extreme sport.

Love the water? Try scuba diving, wakeboarding, waterskiing, or kitesurfing. Want to see things through a bird's-eye view? Try rock or wall climbing, skydiving, bungee jumping, or parasailing. If you want to stay closer to the ground, try BMX bicycling, trail running, in-line skating, skateboarding, or paintballing. You might even try riding a motorcycle—with training and a helmet, of course.

No matter what you pick, you'll get the adrenaline flowing and get some exercise in!

Add Some Green to Your Wardrobe

Although red is a signature Aries color, green is also in harmony with Aries's season: spring. Shades of green that are in alignment with nature—such as grass green, emerald, and sage—are especially complementary.

Spruce up your spring wardrobe with some of these greens, whether as full pieces or accents like jewelry or pocket squares. The color will remind you of your special season, and help motivate you to focus on new beginnings and growth.

Wear Comfortable Shoes

As an Aries you're always on the go—and you're going fast. You don't need fancy, uncomfortable shoes slowing you down, so opt for sneakers whenever you can. You'll be agile, and your feet will be grateful for the support. If you really must wear something more dressy, only wear shoes you could run in at a moment's notice. Many shoe brands today offer comfort *and* modern designs—look around for some options that will work for both your fashion sense and lifestyle.

Host an Island Party

When you need to kick back and have some fun, host an island party with your friends! Create a signature drink (with paper umbrellas, of course), and serve themed appetizers like jerk chicken bites, coconut shrimp, or grilled pineapple. For entertainment add some music and dancing. Steel is an Aries metal, so cue up some infectious steel drum band music and lead a conga line. The percussive beat is energizing, and leading a bunch of people will make Aries feel confident and happy.

Lead Others

When you practice regular self-care, you'll likely find that you have more energy that you want to give to others. In fact one of Aries's missions in life is to inspire others, so look for ways to incorporate leadership into your life.

Whether it's mentoring a colleague at work, encouraging others to join a volunteer effort for a cause you're passionate about, or inviting friends to practice various self-care methods, you can lead others with your Aries sense of adventure. You'll feel rewarded by all the positive outcomes you'll see from your efforts.

Practice the Warrior Pose

Aries is ruled by Mars, the god of war, so it follows that the Warrior Pose would be perfect for his sensibilities. This strong, fierce yoga pose improves balance and strengthens your shoulders, back, and legs.

From a standing position, bend one knee 90 degrees (keep your knee over your ankle) and push the other leg far out behind you, with the sole of your foot on the ground and your back foot placed perpendicular to your front foot. Raise your arms straight up into the air with your palms facing each other, and look up to the sky. Breathe deeply.

Rediscover Your Power with a Bloodstone

Crystals and stones carry amazing powers from the earth. Bloodstone, a black, gray, and red gemstone, is known for its ability to restore your body and rebalance your mind. Bloodstone is also connected to Mars, and holding it in your left hand while you meditate will make you especially powerful. (The left side of the body including the left hand receives energy. The right side discharges energy. When you hold a crystal in the left hand, you receive the mineral's benefits.) Take deep breaths for several minutes, or recite a mantra that resonates with you. You can purchase this stone in a raw form, or polished in various types of jewelry or accessories. The raw unpolished form of all crystals and mineral have more energy.

Meditate On the Color Green

An Aries-focused meditation can help bring his seemingly boundless energy and intensity levels down a notch. At least once a week, try spending 15 minutes focusing on the color green, which helps calm this passion and any anger you might have been holding onto. Green is also associated with spring, which is Aries's season and is connected to rebirth and new beginnings. Whether you think of a wide, green meadow or a grassy hillside, allow yourself to de-stress and unwind with this quiet, relaxing imagery.

Pamper Yourself with a Facial

Since Aries rules the head, be sure to take good care of yours with a relaxing facial once in a while. Slow down after a tough workout or a long week of work by visiting a tranquil spa and let yourself relish the soothing hands of a professional spa technician.

Choose the type of facial that's right for you based on your skin type (consider an organic or natural type if possible)—perhaps one that's moisturizing, deep cleansing, or exfoliating. Then sit back and let it work its magic to improve your skin tone and decrease your stress levels.

Recite a Mantra

———————————

Mantras are short, powerful words or phrases that you can recite aloud or silently to yourself to help you focus your energy or set intentions. These words can help you build confidence, align yourself with your passions, or work through a tough time.

The mantra "I pioneer the way" is a particularly effective one for Aries, whose determination and leadership skills are at the forefront every day. Try to repeat it several times a day, either on its own or as part of a meditation practice. Really believe the words as you say them.

Listen to Music

When Aries wants to relax with some music, he might not prefer the quiet strums of a harp. Instead, he finds percussive music to be calming and entertaining. Drum solos and spirited classical music like the *William Tell* Overture will help Aries forget his worries and clear his mind. Create a playlist of this type of music that aligns with your preferences and turn to it when you need to re-center yourself. A 15-minute midday music break can be an especially effective way to disconnect from your tasks for a few minutes before you power through the rest of your day.

Expand Your Reading List

Reading is a wonderful way for Aries to relax. It can also be inspiring and meditative. The next time you're looking for something new to read, consider material that will speak to your Aries soul.

The well-known Robert Frost poem "The Road Not Taken" can serve as your motto. Another poet whose works will resonate with your sense of individuality is Maya Angelou.

If you're looking for something to feed your adventurous spirit, James Patterson's mysteries are well written and thrilling. By reading regularly, you can reduce stress and expand your horizon—a win-win.

Keep Your Eye on Mars

Stay in touch with your ruling planet, Mars. Although Mars is only exceptionally visible once every fifteen years or so, it can be spotted from earth up to 200 times some years since Mars moves very slowly across the sky.

When Mars is close to earth, you'll be able to see a very bright red star. Even when it's further away, though, you can still see the red star, albeit less easily as it won't appear as bright.

Take a moment to pause and enjoy the beauty of your ruling planet. As you gaze upon it, contemplate its energy and take deep, calming breaths. While Aries can sometimes be aggressive, taking time to reflect and focus can restore you to a more peaceful state of mind.

Decorate with Red Geraniums

You may not think of fast-moving, industrious Aries as a much of a gardener, but geraniums are one of the flowers associated with this dynamic sign—and caring for these flowers is a way for you to relax. Don't be afraid to festoon your window boxes and balconies with bright red geraniums to suit your fiery sign. And, if you're worried about getting bored and moving on to another project, don't be too concerned. Geraniums are hardy plants and, while they hate the cold (just like Aries), they are perennials that will come back year after year, especially if they're moved inside during those chilly winter months.

Indulge in a Foot Massage

Aries is always on his feet. When your active lifestyle catches up to you, treat yourself to a healing foot massage.

Whether a professional treatment at a spa or an at-home massage by a loved one, this relaxing treat relieves muscle aches and stress. Consider using a scented massage oil that aligns with your spirit—something bright, bold, and unapologetically energetic.

While this indulgent treatment might not be possible on a daily basis, be sure to care for your feet every day, and make time for a foot massage whenever you can!

Eat a Balanced Breakfast

Aries is always on the go, which makes sitting down to a healthy breakfast somewhat of a chore for this energetic Ram. However, properly fueling your body for what's bound to be a busy day is something Aries can't afford to skip. Plus, as a cardinal sign, anything Aries can do to get himself off to a good start is sure to make his day go more smoothly. The solution is an easy-to-eat breakfast that you can take on the go. Feed your body, and your spirit, with healthy muffins, spicy everything bagels, or cinnamon oatmeal.

Play a Strategic Game

Aries feels restored and rejuvenated when he lets his competitive side come to the forefront. Use your competitive nature to lead you to victory by playing a friendly board game with your friends or family. Just don't take things too far; it is just a game after all.

A simple game may not give Aries all that he needs, however. Aries thrives when he's able to use his above-average ability to strategize as a way to achieve his goals. Save the cooperative games for another day and engage in a fast-moving game of Monopoly or Risk or a mock war video game instead.

Purge Your Belongings

Everyone's home gets a little cluttered sometimes, but Aries hates a mess. Try a Mars-based purge approach and ruthlessly declutter and clean up at the same time. Challenge yourself to fill a trash bag with garbage, and set aside another bag for clothes donations as well as a couple boxes for home goods and book donations.

Deliver the purged goods to the appropriate places so the job is completely finished. Then, once your space is clean, you can take pride in the work that you've done—and enjoy the restorative power of a nice, uncluttered space.

Sponsor a Lamb

You might not have the space or inclination to own a ram (or lamb) yourself, but you can sponsor someone who does—especially someone in need. Look online for reputable charity groups (such as Heifer International) that help connect farmers with sponsors who can help them expand, feed, and take care of their herd. Honor your Aries animal with this act of kindness and generosity that will do your soul good *and* help someone live a better life.

Focus on the Flame

———————

Fire signs are drawn to the sacred element inside them: the flame. From the blue center to the red-hot aura glowing outward, the flame calls you on an instinctual level. Use the power of fire to keep yourself balanced when you need it most. At times of high stress, find a quiet respite. Light a candle of your choosing and sit in front of it. Watch as the flame dances, softly flickering as it burns slowly. Take solace in the beauty of the flame before you, allowing the whole world to fall away around you. It is just you and the flame. Fix your gaze on the flame as it flares and sways, and try to quiet your mind as best as possible. If you find your mind wandering, don't worry. Gently return your focus to the flame in front of you. Repeat for as long as you wish or until the flame has extinguished.

Rest Your Head

Even the most on-the-go Aries needs to stop and rest sometimes. Make sure that rest is as high quality as possible by splurging on a therapeutic pillow to add to your bed. These pillows are designed to support the head and neck while you're sleeping, which helps Aries protect the most important part of his body. Not only does this support relieve physical neck strains, but a good night's sleep also alleviates stress and helps repair and restore the body.

This type of restful, restorative sleep is a vital part of self-care—even for an Aries—so do whatever you can to rest that heavy head and lull yourself off to dreamland as easily as possible.

About the Author

Constance Stellas is an astrologer of Greek heritage with more than twenty-five years of experience. She primarily practices in New York City and counsels a variety of clients, including business CEOs, artists, and scholars. She has been interviewed by *The New York Times*, *Marie Claire*, and *Working Woman*, and has appeared on several New York TV morning shows, featuring regularly on Sirius XM and other national radio programs as well. Constance is the astrologer for *HuffPost* and a regular contributor to Thrive Global. She is also the author of several titles, including *The Astrology Gift Guide*, *Advanced Astrology for Life*, *The Everything® Sex Signs Book*, and the graphic novel series Tree of Keys, as well as coauthor of *The Hidden Power of Everyday Things*. Learn more about Constance at her website, ConstanceStellas.com, or on *Twitter* (@Stellastarguide).